POEMS

Intimate Portrait

Maite Glaría

AMEGLA Publishing

INTIMATE PORTRAIT
First edition, 2024

Editing, Layout
Cover & Back Cover Design:
Anet Melo

©María Teresa Glaría Mejía
(Maite Glaría, 2024)
English Translation:
©Lidice Megla. All Rights Reserved.
©About this edition:
AMEGLA PUBLISHING 2024

ISBN: 9798880021420
Independently published by
AMEGLA Publishing
New York, NY, EE.UU.

$\mathcal{I}$ am my loved ones, those no longer on this plane, and my beloved children and grandchildren, Annabelle, Arlene, Anet, Claudia, and Reynel. Through their loving embrace, I am kept whole and alive by the everyday prodigious strength of their affection. I dedicate this book to them.

Maite Glaría.

Tearing down walls with a flood of verses & hope

Maite Glaría, my friend Máite (with an affectionate accent on the a), has asked me to write the prologue to her fifth collection of poems, *Intimate Portrait*, and here I am, without being versed in matters of poetry. I will try to navigate the depths of the sea of intimacy of a woman whose character is passionate and sweet.

I have read these poems repeatedly to delve beyond words and touch that horizon of love and loss, light and shadow, tenderness and reproach, where Máite dominates her professions of poet, pedagogue, and editor. I have always heard that Poetry must awaken the senses and cultivate emotions. A phrase that might seem corny to many.
Yet, it's cut to size for this woman from Ciego de Avila, who has taken the pulse of life with flavor and joy, thus assuming all her roles: lover, mother, grandmother, friend, and with all of them, she continues to conquer dreams.

From my small standpoint as an improvised reviewer and having read Máite's other poetry collections, I dare say — with no fear of being wrong— that this collection portrays her the most if we agree that writing poetry is the poet's way of portraying the inner world- a selfie in verse.

If in *El ala trunca* (2017) she makes a passionate account of her childhood, adolescence, and youth, already in her following collection of poems, *Amazona de Fuego* (2018), she strips us naked with all her eroticism with poems of a sexuality free of all unhealthy content, purifying in each verse. In *El próximo destino* (2019), we see her reflect on the immigrant's nostalgia and the ploys to redeem her pains, and above all, the longing for an island that, although distant, sustains her poetic skeleton. Her fourth book of poems, *Vientos de otoño* (2020), combines the intensity of a Caribbean hurricane and the freshness of the short, bright days of a woman who flutters between illusion, heartbreak, and rebirth in a body scared by a thousand battles, love, joy, and sadness.

Maite Glaría's poetry reflects a vision of life that is both passionate and reflective. She weaves her verses on themes as old as humanity, such as love and loss, and as current as self-discovery, using emotive and introspective language to capture the depth and complexity of these human experiences.

Hence, it is not surprising that with *Retrato Íntimo/Intimate Portrait*, Máite has come full circle to become the rhapsode of her own epic, recreating herself in the deep exploration of intimacy: love, loss, and identity through introspective and pulsating poems in which each sentence, each word is a flash of sensitivity, like an endearing caress.

The introspective intention is raised since the first poem, "Intimate Portrait," where there is a growing pain/ from the gut, / from the deep furrows/ of silence to the final declaration of "En esta tierra/In this Land," where she proclaims that beyond my roots/ life beats/ and overflows/ in a barrage of verses/ and hopes./ Here the memories/ hatch in Saudades /with the taste of coffee,/ tears and chocolate.

Love and identity are also recurring themes in this collection of poems. A love born of personal experiences and a life nourished by sweet or bitter memories. My friend Máite loves without holding back, and she has no qualms about throwing it to the four winds:

There's a hunger for love.
A whirlwind of cravings,
of longings and desires
throughout the streets
south of Distance.

And in her strength, she can love herself beyond all wounds and adversities, stumbling blocks, and broken paths.

I love my alter ego when she laughs
as if she was a happy woman,
as if sorrows had not left
tattooed scars,

---

[1]Saudade (noun): a longing, melancholy, or nostalgic feeling attributed to the Portuguese or Brazilin temperament specially in their traditional songs.

and the road
wasn't broken,
unstructured,
as if I had not changed shores,
as if my soul knew
where its vessel remained.

A woman who already accepts herself as she is, with
all her imperfections and scars, and her body purified
by the light that emanates from her wounds and
disenchantments, which have made her stronger, wiser,
and more Máite.

It was Françoise Sagan who pointed out that "at a certain
point in life, you want a child. Perhaps, to die a little less
when you die." In "Daughters," Maité Glaria describes
how she could get lost in the darkness, enveloped in gales
of madness and abrupt labyrinths, without knowing where
she is. Her daughters and her family are the anchor that
allows her to weather the storms and find the North Star
in their midst. But I will always find my way back if I
listen to their voices.

The book is structured in five thematic bodies. In the
collection of poems "From the Deep," she grabs the depths
when she asks what love had/been, if it had been at all,
and in "Roots," where Between Deep and Forgotten Roots,
she searches for her source of pain and hope. My friend
Máite is made up of "Spells and Prophecies," like the
violin that invokes / Oshún at dawn,/ the one that anoints
itself / with honey and verbena or appropriates the four
seasons in "Interludes and Seasons," but is flooded by
autumn when the leaves fall / like tears in the soul.
And if you find "Walls" in this book, my friend Maite
Glaría teaches us that we must climb them or knock them
down with a barrage of verses and hopes.

PABLO J. SOCORRO,
Journalist and Writer

from the Depths

I am a naked soul in these verses.
A naked soul that frantic and alone,
leaves its petals scattered.

Alfonsina Storni

Portrait of an intimacy

There is a hurt that grows
in her insides
from the deep trenches of silence.

There is a perennial terror
that makes innocence her own
and it becomes an echo in the
incommensurable abyss
of fear.

There is an absent memory
an intimate agony that clings
to the dead under the broken elements
of her intimacy.

The skin I inhabit

The skin I inhabit,
it's just a piece of memory,
a void in the background,
a taste of Sea in the throat.
Loneliness wears it out,
it folds
and it tears apart.
Once,
a pearly shell at dawn.
Today,
a lizard cooking
under the summer sun.
No dimension or noise,
or promises.
The skin I inhabit is tired,
A lover's late night
that was or was not.
The skin I inhabit, although
in these times,
it's just a shadow,
Dust in the Wind.

How love had been

If with the same strand of time
we had created an endless
thread of new gods,
if we had read Lorca and Vallejo,
and with their verses
created our days,
unraveled the shadows,
if we had
put down roots where no one else
dared leave a mark.
How had it been? Love,
if we had set ourselves far from all the misery.
Me, without the scars on the spine,
watching you shine under the sun,
its filigrees on your body,
birds eating from your hand.
Us, stringing dreams together;
my dreams with your dreams
planting a tree to start a story,
no painful goodbyes or lies.
How had it been
if on snowy mornings
we had seen
the kaleidoscopic light
lacing on the dry branches
and you, warming my cold bones.
How had it been,
Love,
if it only had been!

Beyond

My love goes beyond
sudden death
and the shadows
of the nine circles
of Hell and the abyss
of my own verses.
Beyond orgasm
and its impudent legend
of coveted apple and false
expectations,
(and all the other fruits of evil.)
My love is written on my soul
with light arpeggios.
My love dies and rebirths each time
amazed at the mysteries
of life.
My love is a lake
that nourishes
a thousand passions.
Powerful—and free—,
my love is a pendulum
oscillating
from my heart
to your belly.

Shadows

The shadows on my skin
open wounds,
drown
fond memories,
absorb the light
in my eyes.
They nourish and bleed me.
Silence weighs on me
from the shadows
—A perverted and sullen silence—
like the last spark that agonizes
in my eyes
when the sun turns bitter
and avoiding.
When you leave me with the shadows!
Forsaken,
in pain and darkness,
not a flame, not even that old one
that once blazed within can deliver me
from the shadows now.

I've been looking for you

I've searched for you in the sea,
in the sands,
on both shores of my story,
the glistening shell under the sun
and the wild sound of the shadows,
over the cliffs
where my bones went,
still alive, still stubborn.
I have searched for you
in the unusual place
of the dead,
The Emulator of Dante and Virgil,
tricking Charon,
defying Cerberus and the harpies,
I searched for you in the cracks
of my foolish and useless fancy.
In my hallucinatory verses,
desolate,
in the dark crevice of my centuries-long
loneliness,
but not even at sea,
on my shores,
not on cliffs
or mist,
the emptiness of my perpetual solitude,
where agony escapes my verses.
Nor in the bowels of hell itself
could I find the image of the man I loved!
Not even in his ghost.

Broken heart

From my broken window
I miss you.
You know what they say,
that a broken window brings a direct message:
"There's no one here to take care of this."
Broken, like my heart,
even if it sounds cheesy.
It does. The heart does break.
Yes, it tears,
it leaks, then dries.
No warm blood to feed from,
to hope...

Vesania

There are days when I look for you,
naked sometimes,
or dressed in leaf litter,
ruminating on unfathomable parables.
You've left nothing in me that is not yours.
A thick loneliness that suffers
in the hidden blood of the nights
where my vesania grows,
while demons impatiently wait
for my leftovers for the Aquelarre.

[3]Vesania (Latin) Insanity. Fury.

Just alone

My heart is not tired;
Just filled with an exhausting silence.
A heaviness.
A ceasing of being, perhaps.
The known path,
different now, seems
to lack the scent and
I can't breathe today.
There is a singular emptiness.
A sense of lost soul.
A solitude in the twilight.
My heart is not tired.
I am just alone.

A chunk of city

A chunk of city squeezes my chest today
like a shred of memory wounding me.
it drops itself on my heart
and then chews it.
It wants to annihilate me, but it can't.
I'm still on the edge of the bed,
trying to rearrange my bones together.
This chunk of city
keeps embedding itself in me
and it tortures me.
I reach for the tiny jar nearby,
and put a pill under my tongue,
closing my eyes,
for the chunk of city
to collect every vivid memory
and withdraw.

What to do

What to do with this
tired heart that sometimes,
like an orate goes wild.
Blood itself cannot put a stop
to memory,
and I don't know what else to do
with a love,
that is unforgettable.

(Silence)

Dispersed
the light struggles to enter
my silence whilst
spinning
around this rare and puerile naivety.
A network of memories
that snuggle in my belly,
nesting.
An asylum of disembodied bones.
I've been run over by the rushing light
through that crack of silence
—and I tremble—
I tremble from the memories
I wish not to perpetuate.

(Get to know me)

I am the violin that invokes Oshún
in the early hours of the morning.
The one that anoints herself
with honey
and verbena.
The bow that draws
naked to your spear.
Discover the root
of my brokenness,
the audacity of my sorrows.
My fruit is still ripe,
the almond,
the seed
hard as rock
and the sweet pulp,
like the evening breeze
of my island.
Get to know me,
Love,
before I die.

Alienated

And what do I do now with my soul,
my island-soul,
of sand and sea
and conch shells.
The wind breaks my face.
Distance burns on my skin.
I lose the horizon in my memories
and on dry land,
I wander around, alienated.

A Swallow

A swallow I am
flying over sad verses
where I linger

on my sadness
singing sonnets
over gray skies

in my universe
everything goes dark
if I can't find you.

You Exist

You still exist
in me,
between
my full-of- years
stirred blood
and the memories,
where you grew roots,
like branches that
Time does not want to erase.
Out there,
still
among
the mysteries
and winks of time,
in a parallel dimension
on opposite shores
You exist,
I know it when
I feel you
in the folds
of my skin
alongside
my verses.

Freedom

Sometimes, I wake up
feeling like lying on the ground.
Wanting to spread my roots,
penetrating,
growing this way,
the sap nourishing
the veins
germinating
again, as if reaching
to the sun
was the only thing that existed.
Sometimes, the sea, with its artifice
goes through me.
Its waves languish
on my skin already foamed
and then I lie on the sand
which is also
part of this Earth;
Immense Paradise,
Freedom With No Borders.

of *Spells*
& *prophecies*

I sell you this prophecy:
you, at night, in your dreams,
will dream that you loved me...

Rafael de León

Prophecy

Slowly approaching
the divine warmth of Dawn
we shall touch when my kisses reach you.
Two ears of grain,
a delusional binomial,
Honey,
Aroma,
Fire and Fantasy.
No more shipwrecks.
Slowly approaching,
embrace me with your nights.
Dispel nostalgia.
Then, volcanoes shall fall dormant,
Rain, its coven shall dampen,
Tenderness will disclose a new horizon,
and our prophecy shall be fulfilled.

Spell

A Strand of Moon
enchanting tonight,
diaphanous bark
of coiled branches,
fertile sleep
I want to nest in you,
become lamp
radiance or stem.
But I'm a flower,
root and fruit,
conch shell and foam.
My memory,
a silent angel.
In the mornings
overwhelmed, I wake
by the threads of light,
laboriously weaving
into my body,
the fate of two.

Doors

Behind each door,
A hidden challenge,
A scream,
Hope,
An endearing voice
calling memories.
A blue threshold
opening in time,
and there is no pain
or distance through it.
Grandmother's embrace
behind the door,
awaits.
That door of infinite love, then,
opens towards the homeland.

if (I found you)

If by that grace of fate that sometimes
unfolds before us
when the wind wanders and makes us lucky,
I found you one day,
you'd be sitting in one of those petite cafés
by sidewalks full of light - from the sun or from
streetlamps—
it matters not,
your cottony hair would be sticking out,
above the book you're reading
and you'd realize that I'm there,
like a lost bird
insignificant, just a wet dove
foreshadowing.
And you'll realize I've come from afar for you to
read me a poem,
—one, where I'd fit in —if you were to notice me.
But how can I find you?
Where, if I do not venture beyond the shores of
my own shadow.
... I dig up stories that I've lived and others that
I haven't...
—not with you, anyway.

Stay

Stay where you are.
Don't walk away,
Death is not the end; it is all beginnings.
Listen to the sea's designs.
The illusion behind the shadows.
Stay where you are.
Let Dawn find you
and caress your hair.
It's not the end, but all beginnings.
Life's a torrent, an avalanche
of moments
breaking up into chimeras,
I still can't find the way out
this labyrinth that weighs down,
only stumbles
at the edge of my own abyss,
in this darkness that haunts me.
Yet, stay,
I still have memories
to adorn your body with.
Stay where you are, Love.
In case I come back.

Hunger for Love

There's a hunger for love.
A whirlwind of cravings,
of longings and desires
throughout the streets
south of Distance.
There is a never-ending attachment to dreams
from a time
when everything was from the sea,
fervid and luminous.
A hunger for love
in the dark evenings
of a park in shadows.
And next to hunger,
a memory pain
rushing into time,
distance,
desires,
and shadows.

I love my Alter Ego

I love my alter ego when she laughs
as if she was a happy woman,
as if sorrows had not left
tattooed scars,
and the road
wasn't broken,
unstructured,
as if I had not changed shores,
as if my soul knew
where its vessel remained.

Age

I am bitten by this agony-with-winter-edges
that's already getting old.
Like strands of sunshine, they fight
the afternoon's abandonment,
amalgamated with fireflies,
biting my heart in its rapture.
And I only hope to defeat the wolves of the night.

So I don't forget you

If only I could remember your mouth.
Your mouth, scarred by a hundred
hungers in that place of nameless sorrow.
A harbor as bitter as the truths
in a broken home.
Your mouth when it suffered from insomnia
with a certain candor in the mornings.
Your mouth of silence turned into light.
If only I could not forget that your mouth
was a torn heart,
a river of blood and shadow.
If only you had left me the scar of a kiss
that would not let me forget you.

Yield

I want to accept reason's summons.
Leave all eagerness behind,
all longing,
return within me and
stay there.
Shelter the self.
In my bones.
No more heartaches.
No more misgivings.
Come what may,
I embrace what's left
and what I have now.
I give up my wings,
I erase uncertainty.
I empty my cup
of all wine
and without expectations,
meet my destiny.

Faith

I am amazed at our ability
to weather storms;
so much pain and shadow.
How can the heart
—tired of his own suffering—
continue to beat at the sight of such great
miseries?
How can the mouth crack a smile
when a grimace of pain clings to it.
When tears struggle, their flow
contained, and they rebel
in an act of sudden audacity,
to turn the nose into a waterfall
of uncontrollable crying?
Then,
the heart is unbridled in its bitterness,
frightened at the eyes of death,
then, we pray to God that we
may find comfort.

One hope

There is an urgency hidden in the walls.
A sob in the memory of my lineage.
There is a gale of dreams bothering
time and memory.
Dusk hangs over my unprotected loneliness.
There are shadows that make up the agony of
not seeing you,
and they make me a fragile specter of the past
Yet, in autumn
one hope remains: Your hands.
Your hands that hold my sadness
at the edge of my deranged heart.

To be a Conch Shell

I'm going to the sea.
I always go to the sea
when I want to get away from the mist
that muddies and leaves me inert.
So, to the sea, I go,
to draw from its freedom, its infinity.
Ah, the sea!
Exalting Brackish Aroma!
Moist Mantle.
Tears of Souls.
Your waves,
Scimitars, wounding unmistakable concert,
Old,
New,
Sea...
My feet foam
and the throat burns from all the salt.
Still, tempted by your
blue
and green
grey
and black loneliness,
I give myself you.
Oh, Sea!
I want to rest within you.
Accept fully.
To that city of shadows, I belong no more.
No longer hatred and chimeras.
No longer the pain of seeing that which walks
away.
Take me, Sea,
in your embrace.
I wanted to be light, and I could not.
I chose to be a conch shell, then.

Anew

When you feel
the cycle of life
closing in on you,
that there is
nothing else to do
with your mornings
and your weary afternoons,
when you think new shoots
will no longer sprout in your yard
and that kiss, you cannot forget
it's already far away, then
by those unfathomable
mysteries of life,
a new light shines on your doorstep.

Before I go

You smell of bliss
of wet grass
of honey,
and azucena[4].
Of snow freshly fallen.
You smell like the sea,
like my land's burning sand.
Your smell perfumes my way.
I look for you across the horizon
to find you, at last,
before I go.

---

[4]Azucena: Spanish word for Lily, specifically the Madonna Lily.

At the end

At the end of my memories, I enter,
a thousand enigmas invading my bones.
The sun on my plexus burns.
No wails to muddy the free and warm thicket
of my memories.
Not a disturbance in my exhausted heart,
Not a particle to condemn me.
Bare feet, I brake,
Hands cleansed,
Head high.
No longer troubled by
the weary heart,
the weakened legs,
the swollen veins...How could I?
Only this morning, new Gardenias bloomed!

Interludes & Seasons

The Time of our bodies,
with their wounds and traps...

Ernesto R. Del Valle

Opposing seasons

If a piece of Winter
were to arrive
this Summer,
cravings,
longings
would wake.
A good omen
for the souls
that yearn to bind
beyond opposing seasons.
Same way
love binds
beyond sea,
fire,
distance,
and oblivion,
memory,
bones,
skin,
and tears.

Allies

The rain and the cold
seem to have become
nostalgia's allies,
the cold hurts.
It catches you
freezing your dreams
making them strange
(as if they were not yours),
unattainable.
And the rain believes
—candidly— it can
cleanse you of sadness.

Fog

It's a foggy day, true.
And fog is a lot like sadness.
Yet, these drops falling,
before dying, bring hope.
Permeating with sounds
to gladden the soul of all dry souls.
Wanting to bring them to the light,
even if it's foggy, yes.
True, that is a foggy day.
Yet, sadness, too, shall pass.

The Cathedral of the Sun

The cathedral of the sun is pure magic
when uncovered in the night of dreams.
Raised above fears,
the cathedral of the sun opens paths,
welcomes the suffering,
those who love without fear,
those who do no harm
and embrace the good.
There is no evil in it.
The cathedral of the sun
it's for those who wear,
on their hearts,
a star.

Seed

The sea that surrenders to the ocean,
fascinated by its greatness
and the force that animates it,
overlooks the inner river
that silently flows inwardly
thus, infatuated, plants there,
in the lush and fertile,
its seed.

Today

Today, the cold invades the desolate heart,
squeezing,
it dries it out.
It extracts the sweetness from it,
and leaves it bloodless.
The pigeons — mercilessly
peck at the amalgamated leftover flakes
scattered over the frozen corners.
Today, the cold seeps through the open wounds.
Today, the cold turns blood into stone.

Spring

I

The hearth burning in the living room
sparks bells fading into winter.
Spring is coming.
Time to spread my wings.

Divine Spring,
whereupon the birds nest,
and the earth births flowers;
songs,
odes of love and harmony,
sonnets, glosses, and romances,
my soul crafts to get to your kisses.

II

Seductive
Sensual
May
Spring
Bunches of lilies
Gardenias
Sprouts
the juicy fruit
and the jubilant bird
on the hedge.
Splendor,
reminiscing our first
stolen kisses,
under the stairs...

Summer

I

Get closer to love
this summer.
Its endeavor will deliver
your bonds.
The warmth
of the auroras
will emerge
with new energy.
Be
like a spike
or a
delirious
binomial
 the aroma
of fire
and honey.
Get closer to love.
No more
shipwrecks.
Only then shall the
Volcanoes
and the rain slowed down their coven.

II

The summer rain feeds me
as if every drop were essence
that nourished me and bound me to the
universe.
I am alone.
The rain pouring down
on my cravings.
Delirious comes to my memories
the ghost of lost youth.
My mother paints pictures on the canvas of
time,
I shall fill my emptiness with them.
Fueled by this rain
that dresses me up with
the power it engenders.
Caressing the rain
its smell,
its signature
on the mother-of-pearl
cast by the moon that decorates
the branches of the night,
when it rains.

III

Summer evenings stir me up.
Fill me with memories;
an eagerness
so proud,
so passive,
exhausting.
Summer evenings,
Voluptuous
Wet
Stirring
Warmth, these afternoons
overwhelm
overflow into the atrium
Desires
And my body,
with them.

Autumn

I

Gripped by this luminous autumn
where the sky takes the tone
of perennial sunset,
I surrender to the hug
of its ochre branches
they embrace me,
keep me warm
and nurtured.
Nourished by the warm sap of this fall,
I moan happily, a kid
trapped in dreams
of childhood.

II

If you were here
on this autumn day
that just dawned
intertwined
to this mind-blowing trail
of purple and scarlet leaves
from where you to look at me
and I can only see you,
as usual,
so far away...

III

Flooded by autumn.
It spreads its wings before me.
Leaves fall
Like tears on the soul.

Autumn
on my silvery roots.
Golden Omen
that hugs me.
Strands of light,
glimmers of hope.

IV

Autumn, leave me the golden sap,
the whirlwind of leaf litter streams
to take me to the sea.
The golden sea of remembrance!
Let the byproduct of tiredness turn
my veins ochre
let it be carried in me.
And that I turn into leaves
whether fell or
pushed by the wind
be the magnitude
of the sacrifice
to get lost, alone
into this autum,
between my tears...

Winter

I

Winter feeds on my sadness,
smells the animal that dwells within
giving me away.
It rips my heart out
and it feeds off it.
Slashing the voice that bursts within,
lurking in the throat,
it turns me into hard meat; it shrouds me.
Oh, if I could
—without bone and tongue drying up—
pull the strings of winter,
the space where my sadness dwells,
the corners of oblivion
and the stifled weeping of memory.

II

And when the snow danced with the sun
once upon a winter,
dry leaves weaved garlands on my hair.
The afternoon turned amber,
its ice prisms tattooed on my skin,
their arabesques.

III

The winter cold
devours me
as you approach
with your distant lament
of unscented flowers
and twisted words.
No longer do I let
the rain through
my sadness.
Nothing about you
affects now.
Our song
you no longer play it.
And your fingers are
just grey powder
over my memory.

IV

Desolate,
Winter already scares away.
Greening the trees, it let go.
Flowers bloom
and it still wants to
hold them with its flakes,
dress them up.
It swirls.
Dissenting.
It wants to stay, yet
struggles.
Leaving is always tough.
So, it settles in loops,
stiffing
off destiny.
Stiff, yes,
like my anguish.
True, it weakens now,
but it's still got a fight within.

V

January brings
a new sun
a renewed hope
into the helpless bosom
of the afternoon.
The snow
crunches under my feet
with the hidden
verse I lost
back in my homeland
where January
might not bring
a new sun,
only maybe,
some hope.

VI

I carry you inside
woven into me
like ivy
on the deep wall
of dreams.
In me, like a tidal wave,
the blooming of stars.
A gift,
a flutter of crows.
I've got you inside
in the dark labyrinth
of memories,
lights, and shadows,
like stained glass.
In garlands like
Mysteries,
I carry you within me,
Solitude,
like winter does.

Walls

A wall I'm looking for a wall of granite
Where the sea of your infinity crashes.

Dulce María Loynaz

A wall

In the shade,
in the grey shade of memories
I've been building
a wall.
Erecting wall
of all my doubts and atavisms,
respecting my inner
understanding,
my failures.
A blind wall that leaves out.
Instead of stones and wailing,
my own pillars.
A wall that keeps me away
from the stubborn process
of dying.

Naked

Before the eyes of silence, naked.
Verses,
like strings of a violin torn apart.
I try to hide such misfortune
next to my tears and bones
but a dense opacity envelops
and my blood spills irrepressibly,
flowing in agony toward death.
I'm naked in the face of a sick land.
I've lost my way,
and I breathe
—though I don't know if I can—
through the unfinished hole of insecurity.

Why

If there is a strand
of memory left in you,
I will remind you that my love
was your homeland,
your path, your hope;
"A gift from the gods", you used to say,
when you sheltered your longings in my bosom,
when your mouth still muttering with delirium
whispered intimacies on my back.
Together we were destiny and glory,
hearth and flame.
And now I say, "Love"
and you say, "Stop."

Penury

Years have not made her more serene
or more prudent.
They have not made her more sensible.
Tranquility does not count for her,
even less so now that time
becomes an impalpable cloud
fleeting.
In her thoughts.
A specter of shadows has appeared,
it does not let the light through
and she needs light
to get her bearings.
Days become vain spaces.
Clumsy.
Fractured joy
escapes through the cracks,
sustenance evaporates
and there is always an unsatiated hunger,
an unexpected cold penury,
yet this is not about gratifying eating,
or breathing,
but about retaining
—within this absurd being—
the longing for a love that is no longer.

Absence

When will I walk again
with wonder intact on my skin?
When will pain stay
on the farthest ridges
of the unknown?
Vague with the singularity
of the broken soul
in a decadent space
of absence,
I lose my compass
before my eyes,
blue, the sea
changes hues
over the forbidden sand
of remembrance.

On the precipice

Everything that overwhelms me
has the fragility
of an overtaken continent
with a reality
that doesn't protect me.
Haunted by artifice,
I find some strength in the verses I cast
to protect me from the prevailing expiry.
In them, my uncertainties surface,
old hobbies,
 they wonder at the unknown,
remote reef, clay
and a blue hope
that takes me away from the precipice, where
—sometimes—
I am tempted by madness.

Avalanche

Avalanche
of feelings
crowding
the dark dusk
shadows of the future
lurking,
and you cannot
close your eyes.
It's all too painful,
the dispossession
of those living
amongst ruin,
they cry, all crying,
even the dogs
when the hungry
and the lonely are silent.
A trail
is crying out for us.
We wonder
if the trail it's good,
if the night has started to clear up,
or if we are just afraid.

Nothing

Ah, Nothingness, old trade,
empty labyrinth,
forgotten squall.
Courageous-less Nothingness.
 Painless, Tearless.
Nothing transcends you, Nothingness.
Nothing transmutes you.
Nor sorrow or pride
leaves flying in a blizzard
that does not bring back memories.
Just Nothing.
No rooster crowing
in the savannah.
Not even a dog barking in the courtyards.
The minstrel sings its own symphony,
yet, no one listens.
Nothing.

(Phantasmagoria)

I've seen a shadow peeking out
down the cliff of my story.
A shadow, a tremulous shadow,
A flood of memories.
Fleeting encounters between sanity
and remoteness.
I have seen its flame
over the memory pile.
Happy and concupiscent love affairs
of another life.
In this one, the shadow that looms
down the cliff of my story is
just a troubled specter,
a phantasmagoria.

Dispossessed

She walks alone
in the early morning.
Her luggage is now light,
just an old book
and a tattered wallet.
There was a time when she
feared owning nothing.
Now, she is not afraid at all,
and now, she has even less.
She sings a song that transmutes her,
her soul exhibits other nuances
under the splendor of her aura.
A new wing has just grown,
behind the broken one,
and she is the happiest in the world
with her old book,
the tattered wallet
and that new light in her eyes
that no longer want for anything else.

Fear

How to exorcise nostalgia?
Oh, wounds that don't heal!
A burst of light is needed
to dilute the shadows,
a bouquet of gardenias
to perfume this loneliness,
sustain this weightlessness.
How scary!
Oh, Songbird, do not go silent!
Let the wall that separates man
from beast stand!

Afflicction

Sometimes, fate
makes my heart grieve
with its sharp darts.
Sometimes, the sea is
not as deep nor enough
to purify my wounds.
Where did my verses soul go?
Sometimes, I am a wraith,
a puerile hunch
a hymn no one sings.
A shadow,
       Nothing.

Melancholy

Melancholy is a torrent
that spreads through the avenues of the body.
It invades your essence,
your dialect,
the root of your inner
concordance.
A cruel bolero.
Unleashed
in the domain of your nights,
no consolation
for the tuning fork of passions.
An animal in heat.
An ambush.

Otherwise

I exchanged a long time ago,
my solitude for books.
Now, they are witnesses to old concerns.
Reflections of the soul's anxiety.
My books belong to so many,
to those who suffer from
misadventure,
strange episodes, such as,
episodes of sweating and laughter
from stirring love
and irrepressible longing.
My books are here, otherwise,
to supply the cravings of living my life.

Roots

And among deep and forgotten roots
I searched for my own source of pain
And I found hope.

Maite Glaría

(They are here)

In my heart,
in the enduring memories.
No heartaches.
With nostalgia.
They're here,
the loved ones
that led before.
I see them in every sprouting
bud,
in the blooming gardenias of summer,
on the blue cliffs,
in my mornings,
in the smile of the stars.
And here, in the memory,
within every cell,
attached to its roots.

Dulce Maria

Dear Mother,
Nothing saddens more than
looking for you today and every one of my days
knowing I will not find you here.
Nor in the living room, nor in the
your old house's patio
where I still see you in my dreams,
where I go,
every night to call your name
even if it still hurts.
Dulce Maria,
sweet and beautiful,
like your name,
I'd sing to you if I were any good at it,
but take these verses instead. They are
simple and humble, as was your life.
If I were granted a wish, Mother,
I would always ask the same one:
To see you, Mother,
and hold you again.

Missing you

Time goes by, and it's always the same,
I always miss you.
There isn't a day
I don't crave your warmth,
your sweet calm.
I miss you, Mother,
on the banks of my arms
and in the consecrated love you gave me.
I miss you so!
Nothing material I can give you any more
for your spirit no longer requires any of this,
but I am safeguarding light and love
on my bosom to gift on your birthday.

(Your home), mother

Mother, I still remember how
you looked at me,
taking my time in front of the mirror,
styling my hair without haste,
Mother, I see you still,
among your butterfly-covered- chrysanthemums.
From afar, you embrace me when the
mockingbird sings
at dawn,
and I evoke your breath when of broken loves I
used lay
covering with my tears
your chest.
I remember your silhouette
in the kitchen, in the living room
by the windowsill.
And I try to find myself again
the course,
the road,
the path to your house;
Home, where the best part of my soul remained.

Spirit of light

Beloved Mother,
the fire of life you gave me
burns in me.
Your spirit of light
calms my sorrows,
sweetens bitterness,
cleanses,
enlightens me.
It transforms
and it perpetuates in me
your loving embrace.

Father

I felt you kissed me, and
I felt Spring with
the moon shining new lights
and the soul laughing.
From the unknown, you approached,
as fragile as the cool breeze,
In the ride of a wave.
Yet, I failed to reach you.
But you kissed me, and it felt natural,
even if it was just a dream,
a necessary memory,
an illusion.

A wink

Sometimes I'm looking for you, father,
in the absent corners,
in the empty spaces
that your silence left me.
I want to enter the labyrinth
at the bottom of my verse,
walk through its passages
without an atom of fear.
I know you are on that side,
unfolding in time,
and though you no longer inhabit your physical
body,
your energy is like a wave
and you peek out, incorporeal
—with a wink—
through the visible cracks
of my stanzas.

Daughters

I could be lost
in the darkness
on the coldest nights
engulfed in gales
of madness,
through infinite gardens
and rugged labyrinths,
not knowing where I am
delusional, confused,
shattered from anguish
in remote places
where bitterness reigns.
Down abysses
with all the ghosts of my days,
dry throat
and icy blood,
but if I hear your voices,
I'll always find
the way back.

Saying goodbye

Saying goodbye is more
than the sum of the accumulated pain over the
years.
It's a seagull lost in the winter.
 A mountain of illusions,
a deception,
a cry.
Saying goodbye
is looking at yourself in an old mirror
while living in disconnected spaces,
the roots to earth, broken.
The water of a river
off to die in the sea,
never recoiling.

Garlands for Earth

Beyond my roots,
Life pulsates
overflowing
in verses
and hopes.
Here, the memories
hatching in Saudades
with the flavor of coffee,
tears and chocolate.
From the pit to the top.
From fear to an I love you,
the orchards are blooming,
hymns have been renewed.
And I, I am weaving garlands
for earth,
to hang my bones
one day from them.

Maite Glaría (María Teresa Glaría Mejía) was born in Ciego de Ávila, Cuba, on September 23, 1952. She has a bachelor's in education in Literature and Spanish from the José Martí University in Camagüey, Cuba. She was a secondary and Adult Education teacher for over twenty years in her country. She graduated from Social Communication, Business Management, Marketing, Public Relations, and Advertising and served as editor and director of the journal Ciencia at the Cuban Academy of Sciences. For several years, she lived and worked in Mexico as an editor and communicator and collaborated on various scientific and cultural projects. She was editor of the *Voces de Hoy* publishing house in Miami.

Maite has published four poetry collections: *El ala trunca* (2017) and *Amazona de Fuego* (2018), both presented in Los Angeles, California; in New York, and Miami, *El Proximo Destino* (2019), dedicated to Cuba, her country of birth, and the 500th anniversary of Havana, and *Vientos de Otoño* (2020). and the collection here, *Intimate Portrait*.

Her poems appear in several anthologies such as La Habana Convida, Miami, mi rincón Querido, and Editorial Primigenios. Cuba poética, and Romance de Luna, Editorial Hispana (USA); Carildeando, Regalo de abuelos, Dibujos Narrados, and Inmortalidad, Editorial Voces de Hoy. Her poetry also appears in two books in the collection of the poet César Curiel: *Flores de Youtan Poluo* and *Pájaro que en su pico lleva la jaula*. She collaborates with poems, narratives, and cultural articles in various publications. Maite has three daughters and two grandchildren, her 'raison d'etre'. She currently resides in the United States.

ABOUT THE TRANSLATOR

Lidice Megla (she/ her) is a Cuban Canadian hyphened poet and translator with several published poetry collections and an international poetry contest winner. She is a 2024 nominee for the Women of Influence Nanaimo (WIN) in the Arts and Culture category. A nature lover and a dedicated translator with a collection ranging from art brut to poetry, fiction, and nonfiction, Lidice is always hard at work in projects that involve and give a voice to those unheard nationwide and around the diaspora. A full member of the Literary Translators Association of Canada and the Federation of Writers of British Columbia.

She lives, works, and learns in Nanaimo, Vancouver Island. Her readers can reach out and find her books in all Amazon markets, or through the url: https://www.amazon.com/stores/author/B07XVT6DK8.

INDEX

Made in the USA
Columbia, SC
26 February 2024

32016902R00057